BABY QUILTS
FOR BEGINNERS

Easy to Make,
Fun to Give

Compiled by Karen M. Burns

D1614051

Baby Quilts for Beginners: Easy to Make, Fun to Give
© 2017 by Martingale & Company®

Martingale®
19021 120th Ave. NE, Ste. 102
Bothell, WA 98011-9511 USA
ShopMartingale.com

Printed in China
22 21 20 19 18 17   8 7 6 5 4 3 2 1

Library of Congress Cataloging-in-Publication Data
is available upon request.

ISBN: 978-1-60468-864-1

MISSION STATEMENT

We empower makers who use fabric and yarn to make life more enjoyable.

CREDITS

PUBLISHER AND
CHIEF VISIONARY OFFICER
Jennifer Erbe Keltner

CONTENT DIRECTOR
Karen Costello Soltys

MANAGING EDITOR
Tina Cook

ACQUISITIONS EDITOR
Karen M. Burns

TECHNICAL WRITER
Debra Finan

COPY EDITOR
Mary Helen Schiltz

DESIGN MANAGER
Adrienne Smitke

PRODUCTION MANAGER
Regina Girard

COVER AND
INTERIOR DESIGNER
Kathy Kotomaimoce

PHOTOGRAPHER
Brent Kane

ILLUSTRATOR
Sandy Huffaker

Contents

Introduction

Few moments inspire the would-be quilter to get out of the "someday" lane and into "I'm ready to do this" mode like the anticipated arrival of a baby. There's a desire to make something personal and one-of-a-kind to welcome this new love in your life. And when it's a new-to-you skill you're trying to learn, it's even better when the gift you're trying to make is one you can start and finish with a sense of accomplishment and style.

That's what we had in mind as we curated this collection of all-new baby quilts for beginner quiltmakers. In these pages, you'll find quilts with the perfect mix of simplicity, ease of construction, and style that are just right for that new little bundle of joy. Simple to piece, with maybe just a hint of appliqué, the projects have easy-to-follow step-by-step instructions. If you want more help with basic quiltmaking techniques, turn to our online resource to find all the how-to you need at ShopMartingale.com/HowtoQuilt.

There's just one difficult thing you'll have to do before you get started on that baby quilt. You've got to choose which one you'd like to make first. Let's get started!

FINISHED QUILT: 42½" × 42½" • FINISHED BLOCK: 21" × 21"

Cuddle Me Tight

BY SUE PFAU •

This quilt will go together lightning fast! Choosing fabrics is super simple, because all you need for the quilt top are fat quarters. So pick out a prepackaged bundle and get started! Sized perfectly for the crib, this quilt is also big enough for a child to cuddle up with as he or she grows.

Materials

Yardage is based on 42"-wide fabric. Fat quarters measure 18" × 21".

1 fat quarter *OR* ¼ yard of green print flannel for squares

10 fat quarters *OR* ten ¼-yard cuts of assorted flannel prints for blocks

½ yard of pink print flannel for binding

2¾ yards of fabric for backing

49" × 49" piece of batting

Cutting

All measurements include ¼" seam allowances.

From the green print, cut:

5 strips, 4" × 18"; crosscut into 20 squares, 4" × 4"

From *each* of 4 print fat quarters, cut:

1 strip, 4" × 21½" (4 total)

1 strip, 4" × 18" (4 total)

From *each* of 4 print fat quarters, cut:

2 strips, 4" × 14½" (8 total)

2 strips, 4" × 7½" (8 total)

From *each* of 2 print fat quarters, cut:

4 strips, 4" × 11" (8 total)

4 squares, 4" × 4" (8 total)

From the pink print, cut:

5 strips, 2½" × 42"

WORKING WITH FLANNEL

Flannel tends to shift and stretch more easily than regular quilting cotton. To avoid a distorted quilt top, pin the pieces together and sew with a walking foot.

Making the Blocks

Press all seam allowances as indicated by the arrows in the illustrations.

1. Sew one green 4" square to one print 4" square to make a pair. Press. Repeat to make a total of eight pairs. Sew two matching pairs together to make a four-patch unit. Press. The unit should measure 7½" square, including seam allowances. Repeat to make a total of four four-patch units.

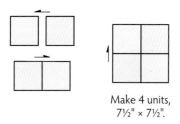

Make 4 units,
7½" × 7½".

2. Sew a contrasting 4" × 7½" strip to the left side of a four-patch unit as shown. Press. The unit should measure 7½" × 11", including seam allowances.

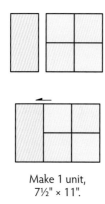

Make 1 unit,
7½" × 11".

3. Sew a green 4" square to the matching 4" × 7½" strip. Press. The pieced strip should measure 4" × 11", including seam allowances.

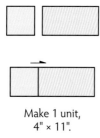

Make 1 unit,
4" × 11".

4. Sew the strip unit to the top of the four-patch unit as shown. Press.

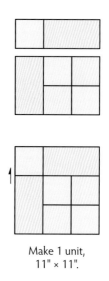

Make 1 unit,
11" × 11".

5. Sew a contrasting 4" × 11" strip to the left side of the unit as shown. Press. Sew a green 4" square to the matching 4" × 11" strip. Press. Sew the strip unit to the top of the unit as shown. Press. The unit should now measure 14½" square, including seam allowances.

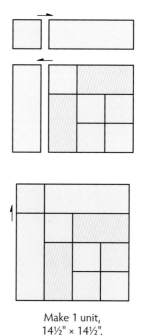

Make 1 unit,
14½" × 14½".

6. Sew a contrasting 4" × 14½" strip to the left side of the unit. Press. Sew a green 4" square to the matching 4" × 14½" strip. Press. Sew the strip unit to the top of the unit as shown. Press. The unit should now measure 18" square, including seam allowances.

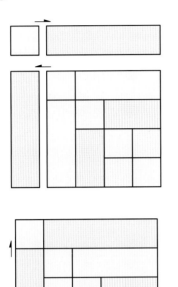

Make 1 unit,
18" × 18".

7. Sew a contrasting 4" × 18" strip to the left side of the unit. Press. Sew the matching 4" × 21½" strip to the top of the unit as shown to make a block. Press. The block should measure 21½" square, including seam allowances.

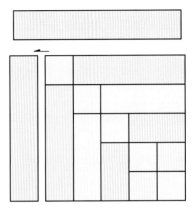

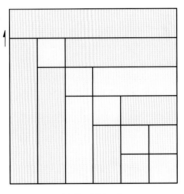

Make 1 block,
21½" × 21½".

8. Repeat steps 1–7 to make a total of four blocks.

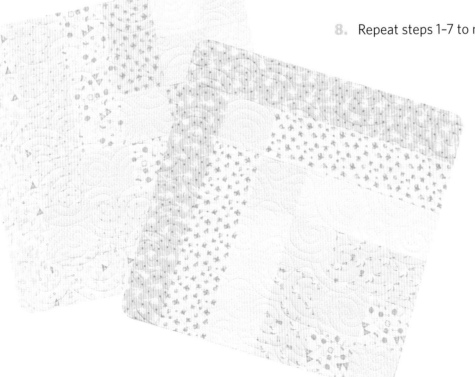

Assembling the Quilt Top

1. Lay out the blocks in two rows of two, rotating the blocks as shown in the quilt assembly diagram below.

2. Sew the blocks together in each row. Press.

3. Sew the rows together. Press.

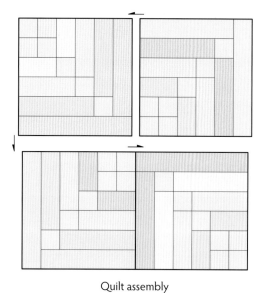

Quilt assembly

Finishing the Quilt

If you need more instructions for any of the following steps, download free information at ShopMartingale.com/HowtoQuilt.

1. Cut the backing fabric into two 1⅜-yard lengths. Remove the selvages and sew the pieces together side by side. Press the seam allowances to one side.

2. Layer and baste the backing, batting, and quilt top. Quilt as desired. The quilt shown is machine quilted with an allover swirl design, which makes a nice counterpoint to the squares and rectangles.

3. Trim the batting and backing even with the edges of the quilt top.

4. Using the pink 2½"-wide strips, make double-fold binding and attach it to the quilt.

HOW TO PIECE A QUILT BACKING

The width of fabric yardage is often too narrow to be used as the backing for a baby quilt. In that case, you'll need more than one length of fabric and will have to join two pieces to make a backing that's at least 4" larger than the quilt top.

The instructions specify how much backing fabric you'll need. For example, if the project calls for 2½ yards, you'll need to cut that fabric into two equal-length pieces (each 1¼ yards or 45" long).

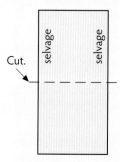

Next, sew these two pieces together side by side (along the selvage edges, not the just-cut edges). Place the selvages together and sew a 1"-wide seam allowance. Then remove the selvages. You can cut them off or snip into the selvages and tear them off. They will tear straight. Either way, you don't want selvages in your backing, as they will not stretch or have the same amount of give as the rest of the fabric.

Press the seam allowances open or to one side and trim the backing to be at least 4" larger than the quilt top.

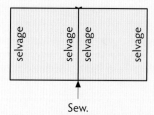

ail Away

BY KIMBERLY JOLLY •

If you're just getting your feet wet with quilting, this easy
project for Baby makes fabric selection a breeze. All you need
is a background, a color for the boat (or bow—see page 16),
and coordinating fabrics for the borders and binding. This is
a perfect opportunity to try out fusible appliqué too.

Materials

*Yardage is based on 42"-wide fabric. Fat quarters
measure 18" × 21". To make the Sweet Bow version on
page 16, substitute pink prints for the turquoise, aqua,
and navy prints listed here. All yardage amounts and
cutting instructions are otherwise the same.*

¾ yard of ivory solid for background

1 fat quarter of turquoise print for sailboat appliqué

¾ yard of aqua print for inner and outer borders

⅜ yard of cream print for middle border

½ yard of navy print for binding

1⅜ yards of fabric for backing

43" × 49" piece of batting

⅓ yard of 18"-wide paper-backed fusible web

Cutting

All measurements include ¼" seam allowances.

From the ivory solid, cut:

1 rectangle, 24½" × 30½"

From the aqua print, cut:

8 strips, 2½" × 42"; crosscut into:

    2 strips, 2½" × 38½"

    2 strips, 2½" × 36½"

    2 strips, 2½" × 30½"

    2 strips, 2½" × 28½"

From the cream print, cut:

4 strips, 2½" × 42"; crosscut into:

    2 strips, 2½" × 34½"

    2 strips, 2½" × 32½"

From the navy print, cut:

5 strips, 2½" × 42"

FINISHED QUILT: 36½" × 42½"

Appliquéing the Quilt Center

1. Trace the appliqué patterns (page 15) onto the paper side of the fusible web. Roughly cut out each shape. Do not remove the paper backing yet.

2. Following the manufacturer's instructions for the fusible web, use your iron to press each paper shape onto the *wrong* side of the turquoise print. Let cool, and then cut out the shapes on the lines.

3. Peel the paper off the back of the appliqué shapes. Referring to the quilt photo, arrange the pieces on the ivory 24½" × 30½" background rectangle, and press. Check to make sure the appliqués are securely attached, and press again if necessary.

4. Stitch around the appliqué edges using a small zigzag stitch or a blanket stitch and matching thread to make the quilt center. The quilt center should measure 24½" × 30½", including seam allowances.

Assembling the Quilt Top

To add each border strip, pin the strip to the quilt at the ends and in the center, and ease to fit as needed. After adding each border strip, press the seam allowances toward the border for a neat and flat quilt top.

1. Sew the aqua 2½" × 30½" border strips to the sides of the quilt center. Press. Sew the aqua 2½" × 28½" border strips to the top and bottom of the quilt center. Press. The quilt top should now measure 28½" × 34½", including seam allowances.

2. Sew the cream 2½" × 34½" border strips to the sides of the quilt center. Press. Sew the cream 2½" × 32½" border strips to the top and bottom of the quilt center. Press. The quilt top should measure 32 ½" × 38½", including seam allowances.

3. Sew the aqua 2½" × 38½" border strips to the sides of the quilt center. Press. Add the aqua 2½" × 36½" border strips to the top and bottom of the quilt center. Press.

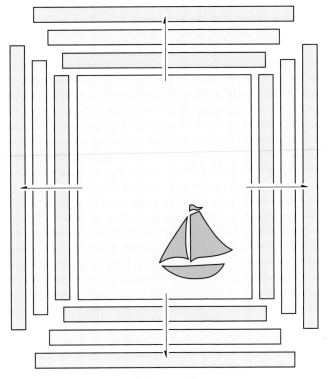

Quilt assembly

Finishing the Quilt

If you need more instructions for any of the following steps, download free information at ShopMartingale.com/HowtoQuilt.

1. Layer and baste the backing, batting, and quilt top. Quilt as desired. The quilt shown is machine quilted with an allover ogee motif.

2. Trim the batting and backing even with the edges of the quilt top.

3. Using the navy 2½"-wide strips, make double-fold binding and attach it to the quilt.

TIPS FOR FIRST-TIME FUSERS

There's no need to be intimidated by appliqué. Using fusible web makes it quick, easy, and fun! Here are some pointers for success:

- Make sure to choose "lightweight" fusible web so that you can sew over it. Heavyweight fusible is not meant for the sewing machine.

- Don't press with your iron for longer than the brand instructions specify. It may seem like a good idea, but in reality, it may make your pieces not adhere.

- Be sure to machine stitch around the edges after the appliqué is in place. For a baby quilt to stand up to repeated machine washing, you'll want to make sure the edges are secure.

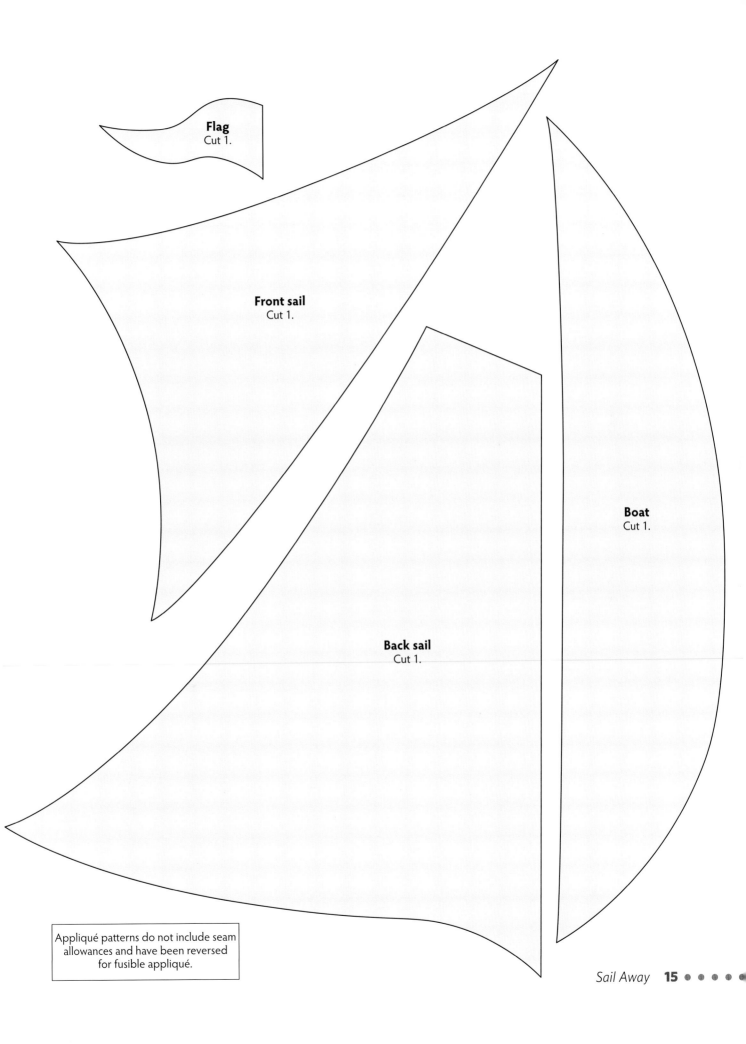

Flag
Cut 1.

Front sail
Cut 1.

Boat
Cut 1.

Back sail
Cut 1.

Appliqué patterns do not include seam allowances and have been reversed for fusible appliqué.

Sweet Bow

Just as fun and easy as Sail Away on page 11,
Sweet Bow is a precious option for any young lass.

FINISHED QUILT: 36½" × 42½"

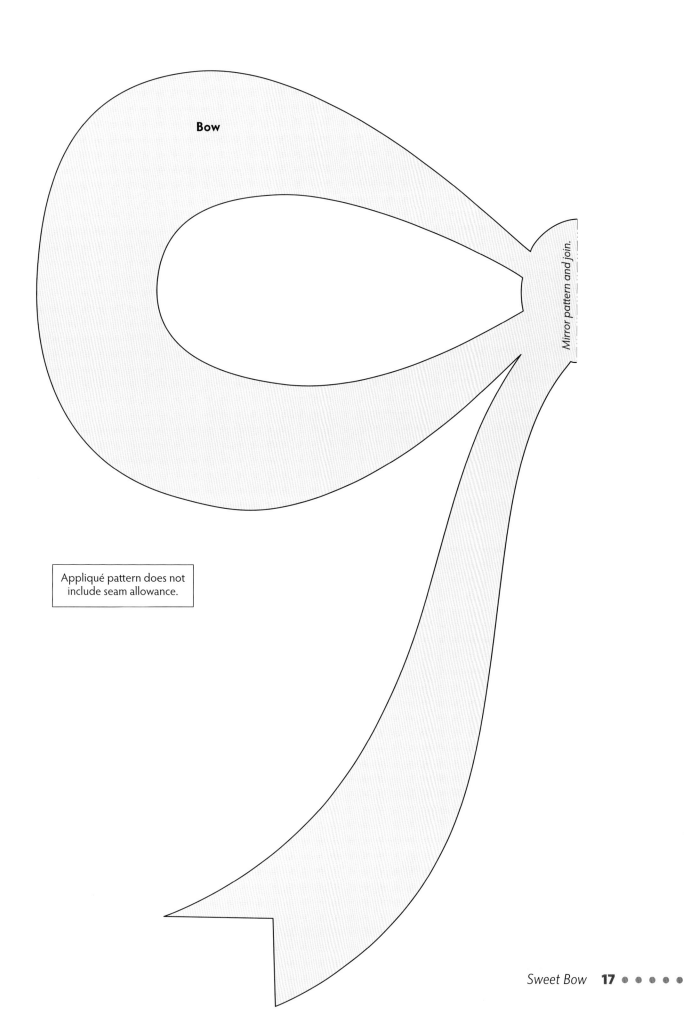

Bow

Mirror pattern and join.

Appliqué pattern does not include seam allowance.

FINISHED QUILT: 45½" × 45½" • FINISHED BLOCK: 15" × 15"

ime to Shine

BY MELISSA CORRY •

Welcome to the world, little one; it's your Time to Shine! Celebrate Baby with this wonderfully modern take on a basic star quilt. With big blocks and lots of white space, this quilt comes together fast and makes a fantastic gift for a new arrival.

Materials

Yardage is based on 42"-wide fabric.

1⅓ yards of cream print for top and bottom panels

⅝ yard of yellow print for star and block backgrounds

½ yard of gray print for stars and block background

½ yard of black print for binding

3 yards of fabric for backing

52" × 52" piece of batting

BACK IT UP!

There are no rules that say a quilt backing must be made from one fabric. Looking to add a little fun? Piece your backing from several prints or leftovers from the front to add interest.

Cutting

All measurements include ¼" seam allowances.

From the cream print, cut on the *lengthwise* grain:

1 rectangle, 20½" × 45½"

1 rectangle, 10½" × 45½"

From the yellow print, cut:

17 squares, 5½" × 5½"

8 squares, 3" × 3"

From the gray print cut:

10 squares, 5½" × 5½"

16 squares, 3" × 3"

From the black print, cut:

5 strips, 2½" × 42"

Making the Blocks

Press all seam allowances as indicated by the arrows in the illustrations.

1. Draw a diagonal line on the wrong side of each yellow and gray 3" square.

2. Place a marked yellow square on one corner of a gray 5½" square, right sides together as shown. Sew on the drawn line. Trim away the excess fabric, leaving a ¼" seam allowance. Press. Repeat on an adjacent corner to make a yellow star-point unit. The unit should measure 5½" square, including seam allowances. Make a total of four yellow star-point units.

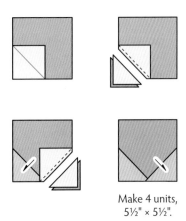

Make 4 units,
5½" × 5½".

3. Repeat step 2 to make eight gray star-point units using gray 3" squares and yellow 5½" squares as shown.

Make 8 units,
5½" × 5½".

4. Lay out the yellow star-point units, four gray 5½" squares, and one yellow 5½" square as shown. Sew the pieces into rows. Press. Sew the rows together to make a yellow-star block. Press. The block should measure 15½" square, including seam allowances.

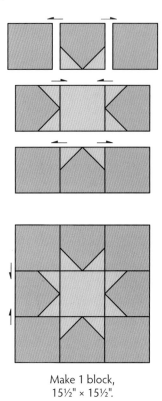

Make 1 block,
15½" × 15½".

5. In the same manner, lay out four gray star-point units, four yellow 5½" squares, and one gray 5½" square as shown. Sew the pieces into rows. Press. Sew the rows together to make a gray-star block. Press. The block should measure 15½" square, including seam allowances. Repeat to make a second block.

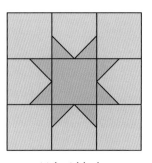

Make 2 blocks,
15½" × 15½".

Assembling the Quilt Top

1. Lay out the blocks and cream rectangles as shown. Sew the blocks into a row. Press.

2. Sew the block row and cream rectangles together. Press.

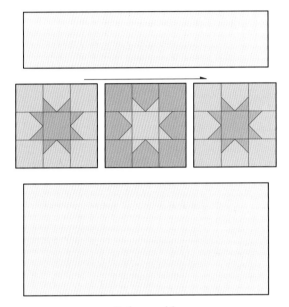

Quilt assembly

Finishing the Quilt

If you need more instructions for any of the following steps, download free information at ShopMartingale.com/HowtoQuilt.

1. Cut the backing fabric into two 1½-yard lengths. Sew the pieces together side by side, referring to "How to Piece a Quilt Backing" on page 10. Press the seam allowances to one side.

2. Layer and baste the backing, batting, and quilt top. Quilt as desired. The quilt shown is quilted in a grid of randomly spaced horizontal and vertical lines.

3. Trim the batting and backing even with the edges of the quilt top.

4. Using the black 2½"-wide strips, make double-fold binding and attach it to the quilt.

FINISHED QUILT: 36½" × 45½" • FINISHED BLOCK: 4½" × 4½"

Charm Pack Shuffle

BY AMY ELLIS •

Charm packs—bundles of 5" squares—are perfect for making baby quilts. This project is easy enough for a beginner, or for the experienced quilter who is in a hurry, since there is very little cutting and just a few straight lines of stitching are needed to make the blocks. Enjoy customizing your quilt with fun fabrics to fit its new owner.

Materials

Yardage is based on 42"-wide fabric.

80 assorted dark print 5" squares (or 2 charm packs with 40 squares each) for blocks

⅜ yard of light print for blocks

½ yard of gray print for binding

1½ yards of fabric for backing

43" × 52" piece of batting

Cutting

All measurements include ¼" seam allowances.

From *each* dark print 5" square, cut:

1 rectangle, 2" × 5" (80 total)

1 rectangle, 3" × 5" (80 total)

From the light print, cut:

2 strips, 5" × 42"; crosscut into 80 strips, 1" × 5"

From the gray print, cut:

5 strips, 2½" × 42"

Making the Blocks

Press all seam allowances as indicated by the arrows in the illustrations.

1. Choose a matching set of dark 2" × 5" and 3" × 5" rectangles.

2. Sew a light strip between the matching rectangles to make a block. Press. The block should measure 5" square, including seam allowances. Repeat to make a total of 80 blocks.

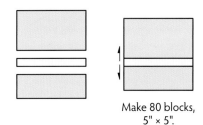

Make 80 blocks, 5" × 5".

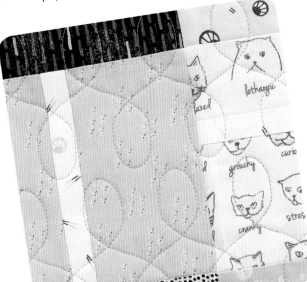

Assembling the Quilt Top

1. Lay out the blocks in 10 rows of eight blocks, rotating them so that the light strips alternate between vertical and horizontal placement.

2. Sew the blocks together in rows. Press.

3. Sew the rows together. Press.

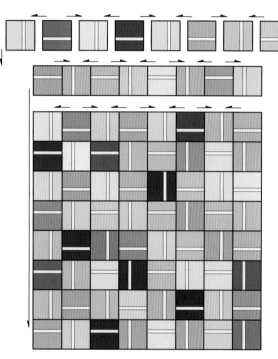

Quilt assembly

THIS WAY AND THAT

Rotating blocks to alternate the position of the light strips makes it easier to join the blocks into rows. You don't have to worry about matching seams!

Finishing the Quilt

If you need more instructions for any of the following steps, download free information at ShopMartingale.com/HowtoQuilt.

1. Layer and baste the backing, batting, and quilt top. Quilt as desired. The quilt shown is machine quilted with horizontal rows of loops.

2. Trim the batting and backing even with the edges of the quilt top.

3. Using the gray 2½"-wide strips, make double-fold binding and attach it to the quilt.

 abyrinth

BY MELISSA CORRY •

If you love precuts, Labyrinth will have you searching for your favorite package of strips to break open. It's made by repeating one easy block and alternating the rotation to create a fun maze effect with lots of movement. Labyrinth will surely keep Baby happy and busy during tummy time.

Materials

Yardage is based on 42"-wide fabric.

32 assorted print 2½" × 42" strips for blocks

½ yard of red print for binding

2½ yards of fabric for backing*

47" × 47" piece of batting

*If your fabric is 44" wide, you may be able to use just 1 length of fabric for the backing, which means you'd need only 1¼ yards rather than 2½ yards.

Cutting

All measurements include ¼" seam allowances.

From *each* of the assorted print strips, cut:

1 rectangle, 2½" × 8½" (32 total)

1 rectangle, 2½" × 6½" (32 total)

1 rectangle, 2½" × 4½" (32 total)

1 square, 2½" × 2½" (32 total)

From *16* of the strip leftovers, cut:

1 rectangle, 2½" × 6½" (16 total)

1 rectangle, 2½" × 4½" (16 total)

From the red print, cut:

5 strips, 2½" × 42"

TREASURED FABRICS

Precut strips streamline the process, but consider adding in a few fabrics cut from family members' old clothing to stitch treasured memories into this quilt.

FINISHED QUILT: 40½" × 40½" • FINISHED BLOCK: 10" × 10"

Making the Blocks

Press all seam allowances as indicated by the arrows in the illustrations. Choose a variety of print pieces for each block for a random, scrappy look.

1. Sew a 2½" square to a 2½" × 8½" rectangle to make one outer unit. Press. The unit should measure 2½" × 10½", including seam allowances. Repeat to make a total of 32 outer units.

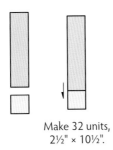

Make 32 units,
2½" × 10½".

2. Sew together a 2½" × 4½" and a 2½" × 6½" rectangle to make one inner unit. Press. The unit should measure 2½" × 10½", including seam allowances. Repeat to make a total of 48 inner units.

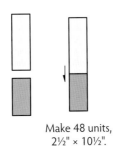

Make 48 units,
2½" × 10½".

3. Lay out three inner units and two outer units as shown, rotating the inner units so that none of the seam allowances align. Sew the units together to make a block. Press. The block should measure 10½" square, including seam allowances. Repeat to make a total of 16 blocks.

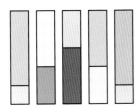 

Make 16 blocks,
10½" × 10½".

Assembling the Quilt Top

1. Lay out the blocks in four rows of four, rotating the blocks as shown.

2. Sew the blocks together into rows. Press.

3. Sew the rows together. Press.

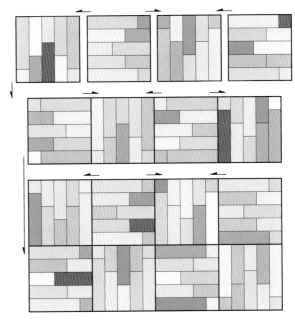

Quilt assembly

Finishing the Quilt

If you need more instructions for any of the following steps, download free information at ShopMartingale.com/HowtoQuilt.

1. Cut the backing fabric into two 1¼-yard lengths. Remove the selvages and sew the pieces together side by side, referring to "How to Piece a Quilt Backing" on page 10. Press the seam allowances to one side.

2. Layer and baste the backing, batting, and quilt top. Quilt as desired. The quilt shown is machine quilted with an allover meandering pattern.

3. Trim the backing and batting even with the edges of the quilt top.

4. Using the red 2½"-wide strips, make double-fold binding and attach it to the quilt.

FINISHED QUILT: 40½" × 40½"

winkle

BY KIM DIEHL; QUILTED BY KAREN BROWN • • • • • • • • • • • • • •

Give Baby's nursery plenty of star power with this supersized double-star quilt. An easy-to-assemble quilt, the quilt top calls for just four fabrics and is equally at home in a boy's or girl's room.

Materials

Yardage is based on 42"-wide fabric.

1¼ yards of bleached muslin for background

⅜ yard of multicolored print for center star

1 yard of red print for outer star

⅓ yard of aqua print for pieced background grid

½ yard of yellow print for binding

2¾ yards of fabric for backing*

47" × 47" piece of batting

If your fabric is 44" wide, you may be able to use just 1 length of fabric for the backing, which means you'd need only 1⅜ yards rather than 2¾ yards.

CHOOSING FABRICS EASILY

When selecting fabrics, here's an easy method to ensure your choices will be successful and blend together beautifully. First, choose any multicolored print you like—this "focus" print means that the work of building a color scheme has already been done for you! Use the colors in this print as a guide for choosing coordinating prints, and your finished quilt will have a cohesive, pulled-together look.

Cutting

All measurements include ¼" seam allowances.

From the bleached muslin, cut:

2 strips, 5½" × 42"; crosscut into:

   4 rectangles, 5½" × 10½"

   4 squares, 5½" × 5½"

6 strips, 5" × 42"; crosscut 2 strips into 16 squares, 5" × 5". Set aside the remaining strips.

From the multicolored print, cut:

1 strip, 11" × 42":

   From one end of this strip, cut 1 square, 10½" × 10½"

   Cut the remainder of the strip in half *lengthwise* to make 2 strips, 5½" × 31½"; crosscut into 8 squares, 5½" × 5½"

From the red print, cut:

3 strips, 10½" × 42"; crosscut into 8 squares, 10½" × 10½"

From the leftover ends of the strips, cut 4 squares, 3½" × 3½"

From the aqua print, cut:

5 strips, 1½" × 42"; crosscut 3 strips into:

   8 rectangles, 1½" × 5"

   4 strips, 1½" × 10½"

   Set aside the remaining 2 strips.

From the yellow print, cut:

5 strips, 2½" × 42"

Making the Center Star Block

Press all seam allowances as indicated by the arrows in the illustrations.

1. Draw a diagonal line on the wrong side of each multicolored 5½" square.

2. Place a multicolored square on one end of a muslin 5½" × 10½" rectangle, right sides together. Sew on the drawn line. Fold the triangle back and align the corner with the corner of the bottom rectangle; press. Lift the top triangle up and trim away the excess layers of fabric beneath it, leaving a ¼" seam allowance. In the same manner, stitch a multicolored square to the opposite end of the muslin rectangle to make a star-point unit. The star-point unit should measure 5½" × 10½", including seam allowances. Repeat to make a total of four star-point units.

Make 4 units,
5½" × 10½".

3. Join the star-point units, the multicolored 10½" square, and four muslin 5½" squares as shown. The Star block should measure 20½" square, including seam allowances.

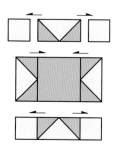 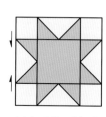

Make 1 Star block,
20½" × 20½".

4. Draw a diagonal line on the wrong side of each red 3½" square. Place a marked square on each corner of the Star block, right sides together. Stitch on the line, then fold over and press. Lift the folded corner and trim away the excess fabric, leaving a ¼" seam allowance. The Center Star block should measure 20½" square, including seam allowances.

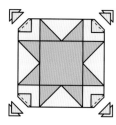 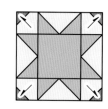

Make 1 Center Star block,
20½" × 20½".

TIP

SURE-FIRE FOLDED CORNERS

When making folded-triangle units like the ones in step 2 above, it's common to stitch the diagonal seam, trim the excess fabric, fold over the triangle, and then press. But Kim Diehl prefers to press before trimming. That way, she says, you can ensure that your corners align before you trim any fabric.

Making the Outer Star Units

1. Sew a muslin 5" × 42" strip to each long side of an aqua 1½" × 42" strip. Press. The strip set should measure 10½" × 42". Repeat to make a second strip set. Cut two 20½"-wide segments from each strip set to make a total of four pieced rectangles. They should measure 10½" × 20½", including seam allowances.

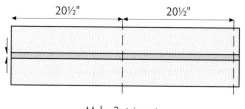
Make 2 strip sets.
Cut 4 segments, 10½" × 20½".

2. Draw a diagonal line on the wrong side of each red 10½" square.

3. Referring to "Making the Center Star Block," step 2, make four star-point units using two marked red squares and one pieced rectangle for each unit. The star-point units should measure 10½" × 20½", including seam allowances.

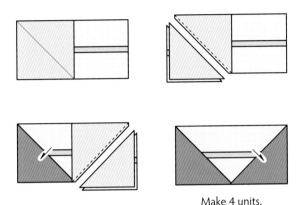

Make 4 units,
10½" × 20½".

4. Sew a muslin 5" square to each long side of an aqua 1½" × 5" rectangle as shown. Press. The pieced rectangle should measure 5" × 10½", including seam allowances. Repeat to make a total of eight pieced rectangles.

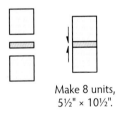

Make 8 units,
5½" × 10½".

5. Sew a pieced rectangle to each long side of an aqua 1½" × 10½" strip as shown to make a square corner unit. Press. The unit should measure 10½" square, including seam allowances. Repeat to make a total of four units.

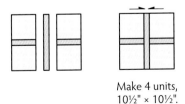

Make 4 units,
10½" × 10½".

Assembling the Quilt Top

1. Lay out the Center Star block, the star-point units, and the corner units in rows as shown.

2. Sew the pieces together in each row. Press.

3. Sew the rows together. Press.

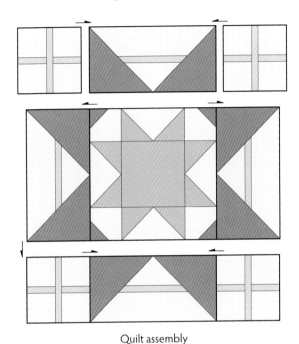

Quilt assembly

Finishing the Quilt

If you need more instructions for any of the following steps, download free information at ShopMartingale.com/HowtoQuilt.

1. Cut the backing into two 1⅜-yard lengths. Sew the pieces together side by side, referring to "How to Piece a Quilt Backing" on page 10. Press the seam allowances to one side.

2. Layer and baste the backing, batting, and quilt top. Quilt as desired. The center block of the quilt shown is quilted with diagonal lines spaced 1" apart. The outer star-point rows are quilted with lines spaced 1" apart and perpendicular to the center star, so they intersect in the outer star corners and form a grid of squares.

3. Trim the batting and backing even with the edges of the quilt top.

4. Using the yellow 2½"-wide strips, make double-fold binding and attach it to the quilt.

FINISHED QUILT: 40½" × 40½" • FINISHED BLOCK: 8" × 8"

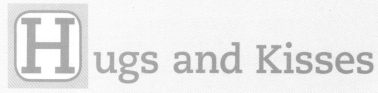

Hugs and Kisses

BY KIMBERLY JOLLY •

Stitch hugs and kisses into a quilt for Baby! Choose eight fat quarters in colors that match the nursery for the easy-to-make X and O blocks.

Materials

Yardage is based on 42"-wide fabric. Fat quarters measure 18" × 21".

1 yard of white solid for background and inner border

4 fat quarters of assorted pink prints for X blocks

4 fat quarters of assorted aqua prints for O blocks

½ yard of gray print for outer border

½ yard of diagonal-print red stripe for binding

2¾ yards of fabric for backing

47" × 47" piece of batting

Cutting

All measurements include ¼" seam allowances.

From the white solid, cut:

1 strip, 4½" × 42"; crosscut into 8 squares, 4½" × 4½"

8 strips, 2½" × 42"; crosscut into 128 squares, 2½" × 2½"

2 strips, 1½" × 34½"

2 strips, 1½" × 32½"

From *each* pink print fat quarter, cut:

8 squares, 4½" x 4½" (32 total)

From *each* aqua print fat quarter, cut:

4 rectangles, 2½" × 8½" (16 total)

4 rectangles, 2½" x 4½" (16 total)

From the gray print, cut:

2 strips, 3½" × 40½"

2 strips, 3½" × 34½"

From the red stripe, cut:

5 strips, 2½" × 42"

Making the Blocks

Press all seam allowances as indicated by the arrows in the illustrations.

1. Draw a diagonal line on the wrong side of each white 2½" square.

2. Place a marked white square on one corner of a pink 4½" square, right sides together as shown. Sew on the drawn line. Trim away the excess fabric, leaving a ¼" seam allowance. Press. Repeat on two more corners to make an X unit. The unit should measure 4½" square, including seam allowances. Repeat to make a total of 32 units.

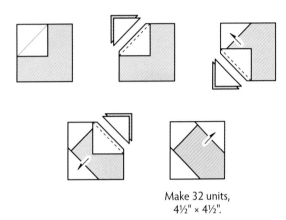

Make 32 units,
4½" × 4½".

3. Lay out four X units, one from each pink print. Sew the units into rows. Press. Sew the rows together to make an X block. Press. The block should measure 8½" square, including seam allowances. Repeat to make a total of eight X blocks.

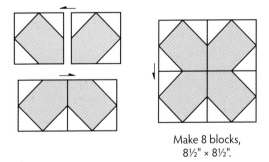

Make 8 blocks,
8½" × 8½".

4. Place a marked white square at each end of an aqua 2½" × 8½" rectangle, right sides together, as shown. Sew on the drawn lines. Trim away the excess fabric, leaving a ¼" seam allowance. Press. The unit should measure 2½" × 8½", including seam allowances. Repeat to make a total of 16 side units.

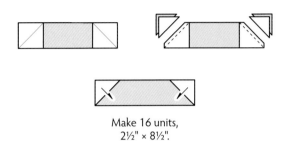

Make 16 units,
2½" × 8½".

5. Sew two matching aqua 2½" × 4½" rectangles and a white 4½" square together to make one center unit as shown. Press. The unit should measure 4½" × 8½", including seam allowances. Repeat to make a total of eight center units.

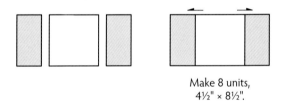

Make 8 units,
4½" × 8½".

6. Sew two side units and one matching center unit together to make an O block. Press. The block should measure 8½" square, including seam allowances. Repeat to make a total of eight O blocks.

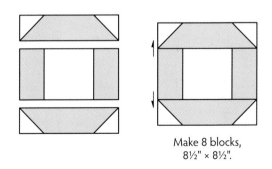

Make 8 blocks,
8½" × 8½".

Assembling the Quilt Top

1. Lay out the blocks in four rows of four as shown in the quilt assembly diagram below.

2. Sew the blocks together into rows. Press.

3. Sew the rows together to make the quilt center. Press. The quilt center should measure 32½" square, including seam allowances.

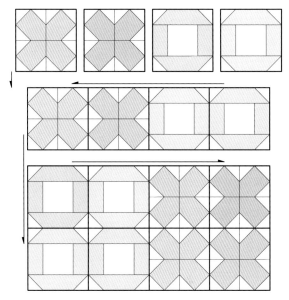

Quilt assembly

4. Sew the white 1½" × 32½" strips to the sides of the quilt center. Press. Sew the white 1½" × 34½" strips to the top and bottom of the quilt center. Press. The quilt should measure 34½" square, including seam allowances.

5. Sew the gray 3½" × 34½" strips to the sides of the quilt. Press. Sew the gray 3½" × 40½" strips to the top and bottom of the quilt. Press. The quilt should measure 40½" square, including seam allowances.

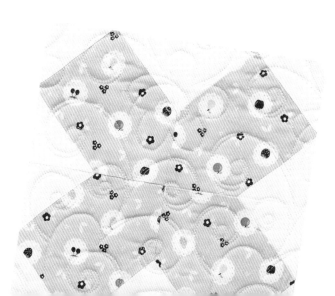

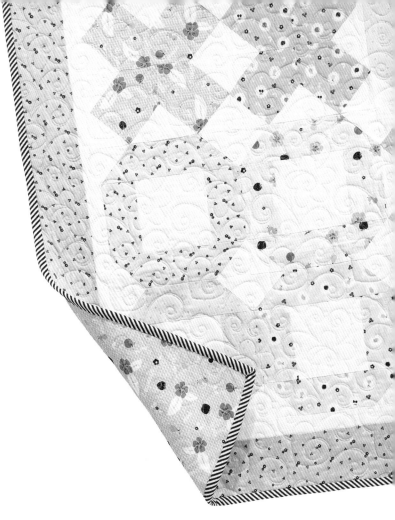

Finishing the Quilt

If you need more instructions for any of the following steps, download free information at ShopMartingale.com/HowtoQuilt.

1. Cut the backing fabric into two 1⅜-yard lengths. Remove the selvages and sew the pieces together side by side, referring to "How to Piece a Quilt Backing" on page 10. Press the seam allowances to one side.

2. Layer and baste the backing, batting, and quilt top. Quilt as desired. The quilt shown is machine quilted in an allover swirl pattern.

3. Trim the batting and backing even with the edges of the quilt top.

4. Using the red stripe 2½"-wide strips, make double-fold binding and attach it to the quilt.

FINISHED QUILT: 45½" × 45½"   ●   FINISHED BLOCK: 15" × 15"

ic Tac

BY KRYSTAL STAHL •

It's easy to choose fabric for this cute baby quilt! Start with one fat quarter in a favorite color, print, or theme, and add eight more, one at a time, that match or coordinate. This is a good place to step out of your comfort zone and throw in a few unexpected fabrics, just for fun!

Materials

Yardage is based on 42"-wide fabric. Fat quarters measure 18" × 21".

9 fat quarters of assorted prints for blocks (Krystal used blues, greens, pinks, reds, and whites)

⅝ yard of white solid for backgrounds in 5 blocks

½ yard of aqua print for backgrounds in 4 blocks

½ yard of peach print for binding

3 yards of fabric for backing

52" × 52" piece of batting

Cutting

All measurements include ¼" seam allowances.

From *each* print fat quarter, cut:

3 squares, 6¼" × 6¼" (27 total); cut each square into quarters diagonally to yield 108 triangles

2 squares, 5⅞" × 5⅞" (18 total)

1 square, 5½" × 5½" (9 total)

From the white solid, cut:

5 squares, 6¼" × 6¼"; cut each square into quarters diagonally to yield 20 triangles

10 squares, 5⅞" × 5⅞"

From the aqua print, cut:

4 squares, 6¼" × 6¼"; cut each square into quarters diagonally to yield 16 triangles

8 squares, 5⅞" × 5⅞"

From the peach print, cut:

5 strips, 2½" × 42"

Making the Blocks

Press all seam allowances as indicated by the arrows in the illustrations.

1. Sort the assorted print squares into nine groups, one group for each block. Each group will include one 5½" square for the block center, eight matching triangles and four contrasting triangles for the hourglass units, and two matching 5⅞" squares for the half-square-triangle units.

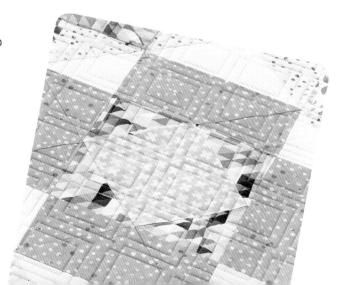

WHAT'S A QUARTER-SQUARE TRIANGLE?

If you're new to making quilts, you may not be familiar with the term *quarter-square triangles*. Quite simply, to make *quarter-square triangles,* you cut a square in half diagonally in one direction (resulting in *half-square triangles*), and then cut it again diagonally in the other direction.

Half-square triangles

Quarter-square triangles

Why choose one over the other? To control where the bias or stretchiest part of the fabric is used in a quilt block. Fabric cut on the bias (the diagonal) stretches more than fabric cut on the straight of grain. So quilters like to control the amount of stretch by sewing the bias edges into the interior of a quilt block, rather than along the outside edge. Once it's sewn to another piece of fabric, the seam helps to stabilize the stretch. If you use bias on the outside of a block, it's easy to stretch the block out of shape before sewing the blocks together.

In this quilt, we're using quarter-square triangles. You cut four from each square, then mix and match them and sew them back together to make a pieced square, where all the bias edges are on the inside of the block and the outer edges remain taut and firm.

2. Draw a diagonal line on the wrong side of each white and aqua 5⅞" square.

3. Choose one block group. Place a marked white square on each of the print 5⅞" squares, right sides together. Sew ¼" from both sides of the drawn line. (If you don't have a ¼" patchwork presser foot, it may be helpful to also mark the two sewing lines.) Cut on the line to make two half-square-triangle units per set of squares (for a total of four half-square-triangle units). Press. The units should measure 5½" square, including seam allowances.

Make 4 half-square-triangle units, 5½" × 5½".

4. Lay out two matching triangles, one contrasting triangle, and one white triangle as shown. Sew the triangles together in pairs. Press. Then sew the triangle pairs together to make an hourglass unit. Press. The unit should measure 5½" square, including seam allowances. Repeat to make a total of four matching hourglass units.

Make 4 hourglass units, 5½" × 5½".

5. Lay out the 5½" center square, the hourglass units, and the half-square-triangle units. Sew the units into rows. Press. Sew the rows together to make a block. Press. The block should measure 15½" square, including seam allowances.

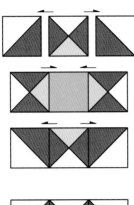

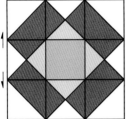

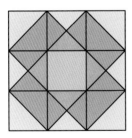

Make 1 block,
15½" × 15½".

6. Repeat steps 3–5 to make a total of five blocks using the marked white squares.

7. In the same manner, make four blocks using the marked aqua 5⅞" squares and the aqua triangles as shown.

Make 4 blocks,
15½" × 15½".

Assembling the Quilt Top

1. Lay out the blocks in three rows of three as shown in the quilt assembly diagram below.

2. Sew the blocks together in each row. Press.

3. Sew the rows together. Press.

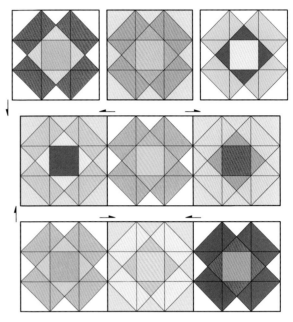

Quilt assembly

Finishing the Quilt

If you need more instructions for any of the following steps, download free information at ShopMartingale.com/HowtoQuilt.

1. Cut the backing fabric into two 1½-yard lengths. Remove the selvages and sew the pieces together side by side, referring to "How to Piece a Quilt Backing" on page 10. Press the seam allowances to one side.

2. Layer and baste the backing, batting, and quilt top. Quilt as desired. The quilt shown is machine quilted with a fun grid pattern that nicely complements the block design.

3. Trim the batting and backing even with the edges of the quilt top.

4. Using the peach 2½"-wide strips, make double-fold binding and attach it to the quilt.

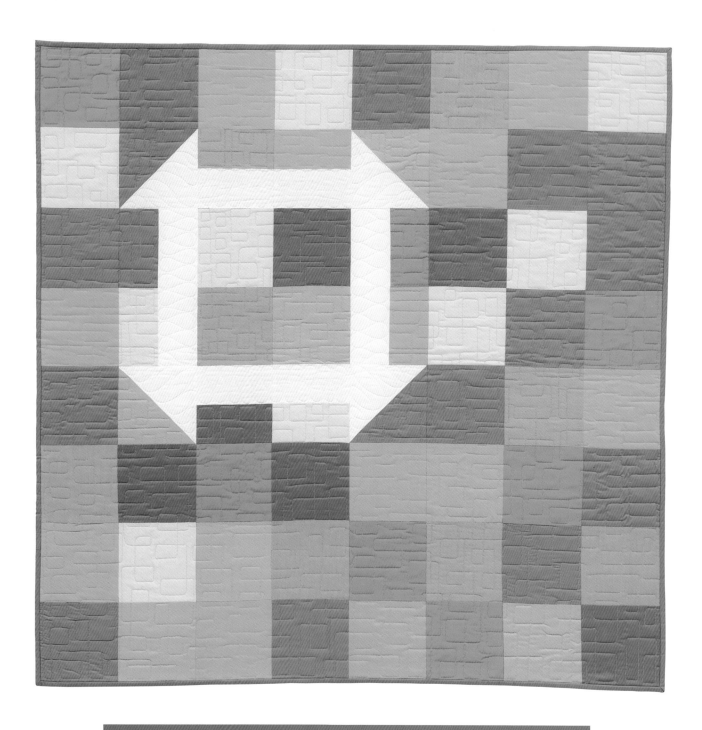

FINISHED QUILT: 40½" × 40½"

Churn Baby Churn

BY VICKI RUEBEL •

Add just the right amount of color to any nursery with this adorable quilt. The versatile design is appealing in solids as well as prints, and is a great way to use up your stash. It's a fun twist on a traditional Churn Dash block that's great for beginners.

Materials

Yardage is based on 42"-wide fabric. Fat quarters measure 18" × 21".

8 fat quarters of assorted aqua and teal solids for squares

1 fat quarter of white solid for Churn Dash block

½ yard of teal solid for binding

2¾ yards of fabric for backing

47" × 47" piece of batting

Cutting

All measurements include ¼" seam allowances.

From the teal and aqua fat quarters, cut a *total* of:

2 squares, 5⅞" × 5⅞"

52 squares, 5½" × 5½"

8 rectangles, 3" × 5½"

From the white solid, cut:

2 squares, 5⅞" × 5⅞"

8 rectangles, 3" × 5½"

From the teal solid for binding, cut:

5 strips, 2½" × 42"

Making the Churn Dash Units

Press all seam allowances as indicated by the arrows in the illustrations.

1. Draw a diagonal line on the wrong side of both white 5⅞" squares. If you don't have a ¼" patchwork presser foot, also mark lines ¼" from both sides of the marked centerline (shown in red below).

2. Place a marked white square on a teal 5⅞" square, right sides together. Sew ¼" from both sides of the drawn centerline. Cut on the line to make two half-square-triangle units. Press. Each unit should measure 5½" square, including seam allowances. Repeat with the remaining white and teal squares to make a total of four half-square-triangle units.

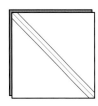 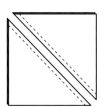

Make 4 units,
5½" × 5½".

Assembling the Quilt Top

1. Lay out the half-square-triangle units, the pieced-square units, and the teal 5½" squares in eight rows of eight as shown.

2. Sew the units and squares into rows. Press.

3. Sew the rows together. Press.

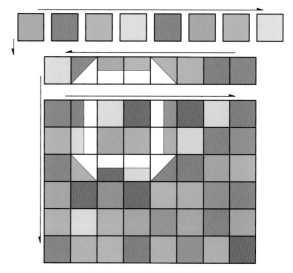

Quilt assembly

Finishing the Quilt

If you need more instructions for any of the following steps, download free information at ShopMartingale.com/HowtoQuilt.

1. Cut the backing fabric into two 1⅜-yard lengths. Remove the selvages and sew the pieces together side by side, referring to "How to Piece a Quilt Backing" on page 10. Press the seam allowances to one side.

2. Layer and baste the backing, batting, and quilt top. Quilt as desired. The quilt shown is machine quilted with a box or square meander pattern. Loops are quilted in the Churn Dash blocks.

3. Trim the backing and batting even with the edges of the quilt top.

4. Using the teal 2½"-wide strips, make double-fold binding and attach it to the quilt.

3. Sew together a white 3" × 5½" rectangle and a teal 3" × 5½" rectangle to make a pieced square as shown. Press. The unit should measure 5½" square, including seam allowances. Repeat to make a total of eight units.

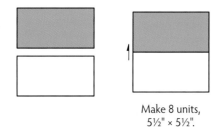

Make 8 units,
5½" × 5½".

Bundle of Joy

BY AMY HAMBERLIN •

Bundle of Joy is easy to make and simple in design, but it makes a bold impact. The key to success is selecting three sharply contrasting fabrics for the background. Machine appliqué the three little words for a sweet (and speedy) finishing touch.

Materials

Yardage is based on 42"-wide fabric. Fat quarters measure 18" × 21".

⅞ yard of navy-and-pink print for background

⅓ yard of dark pink print for background

½ yard of light pink print for background

1 fat quarter of fuchsia solid for appliqués

1 fat quarter of gray solid for background appliqués

½ yard of navy print for binding

2¾ yards of fabric for backing

48" × 52" piece of batting

1 yard of 18"-wide fusible web

Cutting

All measurements include ¼" seam allowances.

From the navy-and-pink print, cut:

8 strips, 3½" × 42"

From the dark pink print, cut:

4 strips, 2" × 42"

From the light pink print, cut:

3 strips, 5½" × 42"

From the navy print, cut:

5 strips, 2½" × 42", for binding

Assembling the Quilt Top

Press all seam allowances as indicated by the arrows in the illustrations.

1. Sew one dark pink strip between two navy-and-pink strips to make one row. Press. The row should measure 8" × 42", including seam allowances. Repeat to make a total of four rows. For best results, start sewing from alternate ends as you add strips.

2. Sew the rows together alternately with the light pink strips. Press.

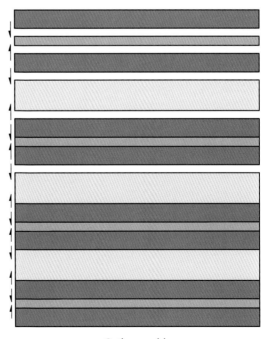

Quilt assembly

FINISHED QUILT: 42" × 45½"

Appliquéing the Quilt Top

1. Join the appliqué *Bundle of Joy* patterns (pages 47–49) to make a complete pattern. Then trace all the appliqué patterns onto the paper side of the fusible web. (The patterns are reversed for use with fusible web.) Note that you'll need two of each pattern—one for the gray background and one for the fuchsia letters. Roughly cut out the shapes. Do not remove the paper backing yet.

2. Following the manufacturer's instructions for the fusible web, use your iron to press the shape onto the *wrong* side of the fuchsia solid. Now cut out the words on the lines, and peel the paper off the back of each shape.

3. In the same manner, apply fusible web to the wrong side of the gray solid. Do not remove the paper backing yet.

4. Arrange the words on the gray solid fat quarter, and press. Check to make sure the appliqué is securely attached, and press again if necessary.

5. Referring to the quilt photo, cut out the gray solid, leaving ¼" to ½" around the words.

6. Remove the paper backing from the gray solid. Arrange the appliqués on the quilt top, and press. Topstitch around the edges of the words and gray solid background using a blanket stitch and matching threads. For more information on fusible appliqué, see "Tips for First-Time Fusers" on page 14 or go to ShopMartingale.com/HowtoQuilt for free illustrated instructions.

ZIGZAG STITCH OPTION

If your sewing machine doesn't have a blanket stitch, substitute a zigzag stitch instead. Sew with one swing of the needle piercing the appliqué and the opposite swing of the needle just piercing the background fabric next to the appliqué shape's edge. No need to overdo it—the stitching doesn't need to be *too* dense, but look nice and hold securely.

Finishing the Quilt

If you need more instructions for any of the following steps, download free information at ShopMartingale.com/HowtoQuilt.

1. Cut the backing fabric into two 1⅜-yard lengths. Remove the selvages and sew the pieces together side by side, referring to "How to Piece a Quilt Backing" on page 10. Press the seam allowances to one side.

2. Layer and baste the backing, batting, and quilt top. Quilt as desired. The quilt shown is machine quilted in horizontal parallel lines.

3. Trim the batting and backing even with the edges of the quilt top.

4. Using the navy 2½"-wide strips, make double-fold binding and attach it to the quilt.

Bundle of Joy Variation

Just as fun and easy as Bundle of Joy on page 44, this version, quilted by Jennifer McClanahan, is a precious option for any wee one.

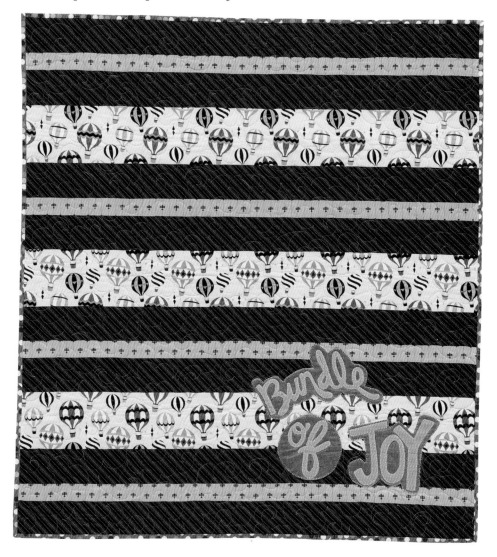

FINISHED QUILT: 42" × 45½"

Join to other half of pattern, below.

Patterns do not include seam allowances and are reversed for fusible appliqué.

Join to other half of pattern, above.

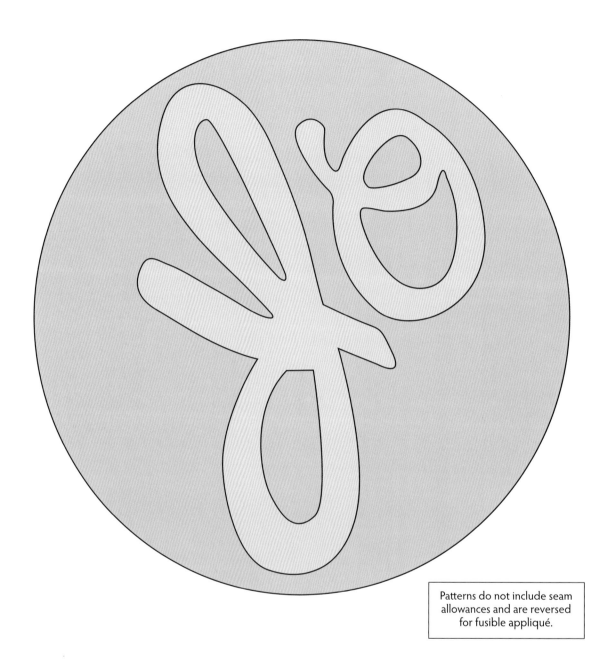

Patterns do not include seam
allowances and are reversed
for fusible appliqué.

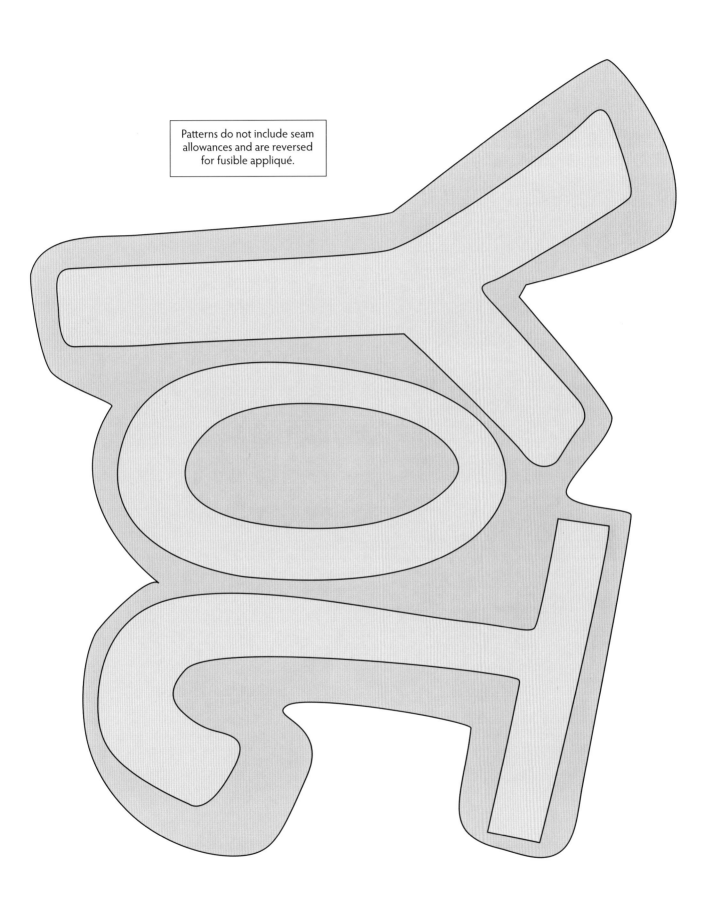

Patterns do not include seam
allowances and are reversed
for fusible appliqué.

FINISHED QUILT: 40½" × 48½" • FINISHED BLOCK: 8" × 8"

Happy Hedgehogs

BY PIPER'S GIRLS ●

Who can resist hedgehogs? Machine appliqué these cute little fellas to delight a small child and perhaps the parents too! Pinwheels, stripes, and polka dots in bright colors add whimsy and make this quilt downright adorable.

Materials

Yardage is based on 42"-wide fabric.

¼ yard *each* of 12 assorted bright prints for pinwheels and appliqués

1½ yards of white print for background

½ yard of black-and-white diagonal stripe for binding

2¾ yards of fabric for backing

47" × 55" piece of batting

1 yard of 18"-wide fusible web (such as Heat 'n Bond Lite)

APPLIQUÉ FABRICS

Use leftover prints from the pinwheels for the Hedgehog and Mushroom blocks. If desired, mix it up by adding scraps of solids (white is suggested for the mushroom dots) for some of the appliqués.

Cutting

All measurements include ¼" seam allowances.

From *each* of the 12 bright prints, cut:

4 squares, 4⅞" × 4⅞" (48 total)

From the white print, cut:

2 strips, 8½" × 42"; crosscut into 6 squares, 8½" × 8½"

6 strips, 4⅞" × 42"; crosscut into 48 squares, 4⅞" × 4⅞"

From the black-and-white stripe, cut:

5 strips, 2½" × 42"

Making the Pinwheel Blocks

Press all seam allowances as indicated by the arrows in the illustrations.

1. Draw a diagonal line on the wrong side of each white 4⅞" square. If you don't have a ¼" patchwork presser foot, also mark lines ¼" from both sides of the marked centerline (shown in red in the illustration on page 52).

3. Lay out four matching half-square-triangle units as shown. Sew the units into rows. Press. Sew the rows together to make a Pinwheel block. Press. The block should measure 8½" square, including seam allowances. Repeat to make a total of 24 blocks.

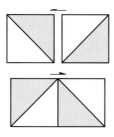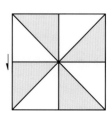

Make 24 blocks,
8½" × 8½".

Making the Appliqué Blocks

1. Trace the appliqué patterns (pages 54 and 55) onto the paper side of the fusible web. Roughly cut out each shape. For the hedgehogs, trace two bodies and two reverse bodies, two faces and two reverse faces, and eight paws (four sets of two). For the mushrooms, trace one and one reverse of both the large and small patterns. Do not remove the paper backing yet.

FLIP THE APPLIQUÉS

It's very easy to change the direction of the hedgehogs and mushrooms. Trace a reverse image of the patterns on a piece of paper using a light box, and then trace the reversed image onto the paper side of the fusible web.

2. Following the manufacturer's instructions for the fusible web, use your iron to press each paper shape onto the wrong side of the remaining bright prints. Now cut out the shapes on the lines.

2. Place a marked white square on a bright 4⅞" square, right sides together. Sew ¼" from both sides of the drawn line. Cut on the line to make two half-square-triangle units. Press. Each unit should measure 4½" square, including seam allowances. Repeat to make a total of 96 units.

Make 96 units,
4½" × 4½".

3. Peel the paper off the back of the appliqué shapes. Referring to the quilt photo on page 50, arrange the pieces on the white 8½" background squares and press. Heat activates the glue, and the appliqué shapes will be fused in place permanently. Check to make sure the appliqués are securely attached, and press again if necessary.

PIN RELEASE

Sometimes it's difficult to grasp the edge of the paper backing to remove it from an appliqué shape. One easy way to release the paper is to use the tip of a straight pin to score an X in the middle of the shape. Slip the pin under the scored area and the edge of the paper will release, giving you a tip to grab on to.

4. If desired, topstitch around all edges of the appliqués using a narrow zigzag stitch or blanket stitch and matching thread. You can add optional embroidery, too. Stitch tiny noses, eyes, and eyebrows to the hedgehogs using embroidery floss and two basic stitches—satin stitch for the nose and eyes and stem stitch for the eyebrows.

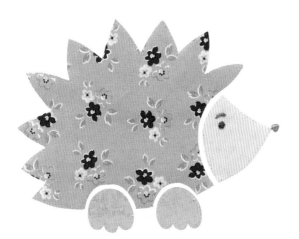

Assembling the Quilt Top

1. Lay out the blocks in six rows of five as shown in the quilt assembly diagram below.

2. Sew the blocks together into rows. Press.

3. Sew the rows together. Press.

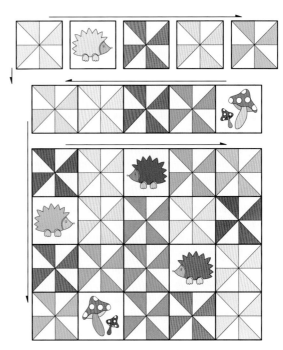

Quilt assembly

Finishing the Quilt

If you need more instructions for any of the following steps, download free information at ShopMartingale.com/HowtoQuilt.

1. Cut the backing fabric into two 1⅜-yard lengths. Remove the selvages and sew the pieces together side by side, referring to "How to Piece a Quilt Backing" on page 10. Press the seam allowances to one side.

2. Layer and baste the backing, batting, and quilt top. Quilt as desired. The quilt shown is machine quilted in the ditch (along the seamlines) and around the appliqué shapes to make them stand out.

3. Trim the batting and backing even with the edges of the quilt top.

4. Using the black-and-white stripe 2½"-wide strips, make double-fold binding and attach it to the quilt.

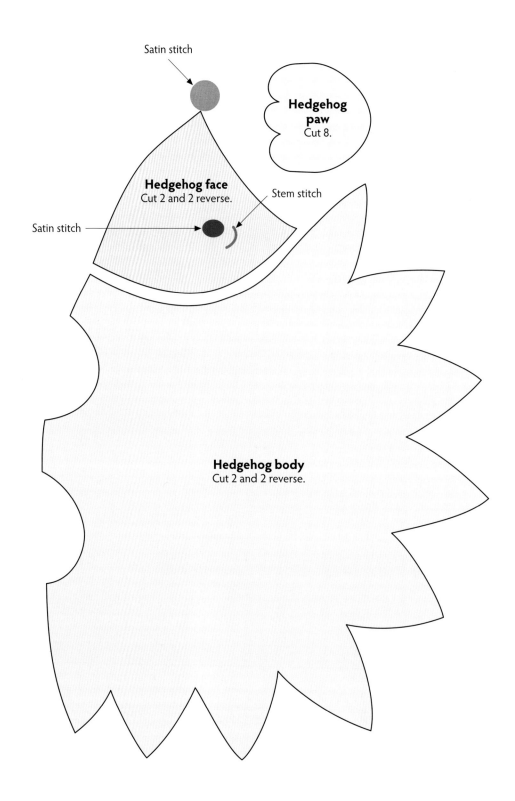

Satin stitch

Hedgehog paw
Cut 8.

Hedgehog face
Cut 2 and 2 reverse.

Stem stitch

Satin stitch

Hedgehog body
Cut 2 and 2 reverse.

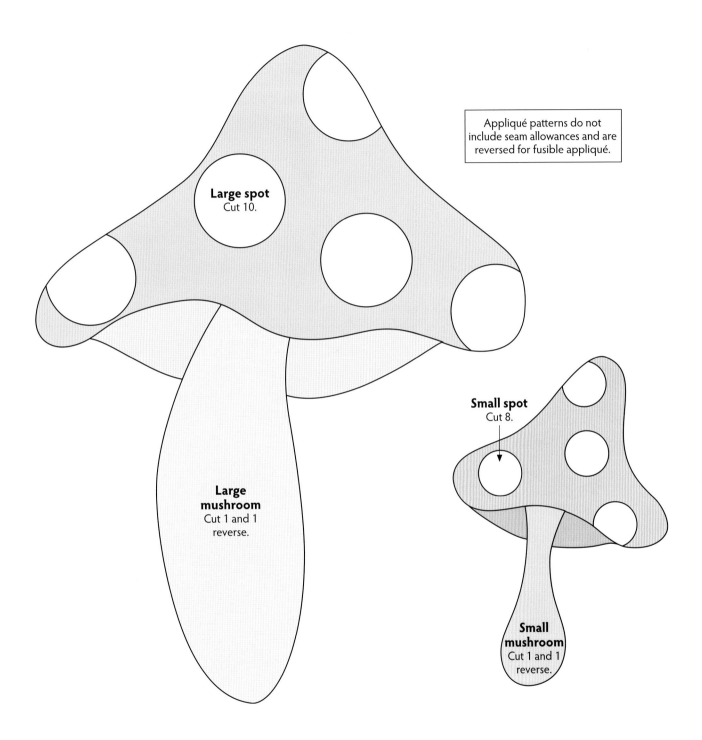

Appliqué patterns do not
include seam allowances and are
reversed for fusible appliqué.

Large spot
Cut 10.

**Large
mushroom**
Cut 1 and 1
reverse.

Small spot
Cut 8.

**Small
mushroom**
Cut 1 and 1
reverse.

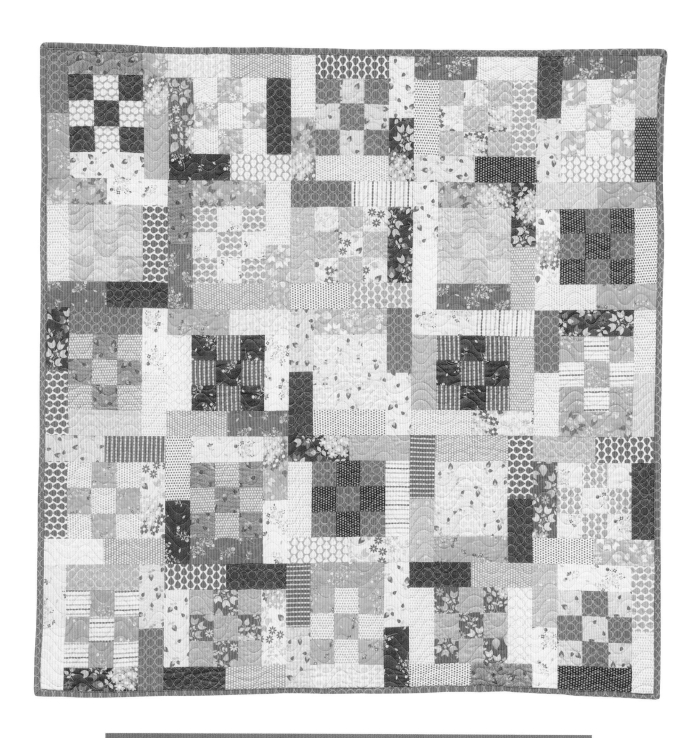

FINISHED QUILT: 50½" × 50½"   ●   FINISHED BLOCK: 10" × 10"

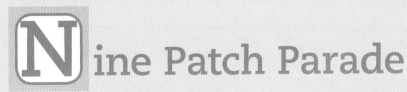

Nine Patch Parade

BY SUE PFAU •

Some of the best patterns are made with precuts and don't require any additional fabric. This quilt is just that! It's scrappy too, so you can't go wrong with color placement. Your family and friends will love your creation and will never know how easy it was to make.

Materials

Yardage is based on 42"-wide fabric.

38 assorted print 2½" × 42" strips for blocks

½ yard of red print for binding

3¼ yards of fabric for backing

57" × 57" piece of batting

Cutting

All measurements include ¼" seam allowances.

From *each of 26* strips, cut:

3 strips, 2½" × 8" (total of 26 sets of 3)

2 rectangles, 2½" × 5½" (52 total)

1 rectangle, 2½" × 6½" (26 total)

From *each of 12* strips, cut:

4 rectangles, 2½" × 5½" (48 total)

2 rectangles, 2½" × 6½" (24 total)

From the red print, cut:

6 strips, 2½" × 42"

Making the Blocks

Press all seam allowances as indicated by the arrows in the illustrations.

1. Choose two contrasting sets of three matching 2½" × 8" strips. Sew the strips together lengthwise to make two strip sets as shown, one with the darker strips on the outside and one with the lighter strips on the outside. Press. Cut each strip set into three 2½"-wide segments.

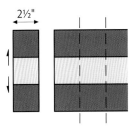

Cut 3 segments.

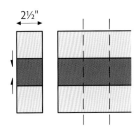

Cut 3 segments.

4. Sew a print 2½" × 6½" rectangle to the top and bottom of a nine-patch unit. Press. Repeat to make a total of 25 units.

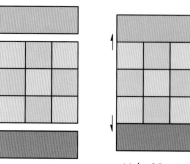

Make 25 units,
6½" × 10½".

CHECK YOUR
SEAM ALLOWANCE

If your nine-patch units are smaller than the 2½" × 6½" rectangles, your seam allowance is too big. Check to see that you are sewing with an accurate ¼" seam allowance. If your nine-patch units are larger than the strips, you can trim the units equally on all sides to make them 6½" square.

2. Repeat step 1 for the remaining sets of matching strips. Keep the matching segments together in sets of six.

3. Sew matching segments together as shown to make two nine-patch units that measure 6½" square, including seam allowances. Press. Repeat to make a total of 25 nine-patch units. (You'll have three extra segments.)

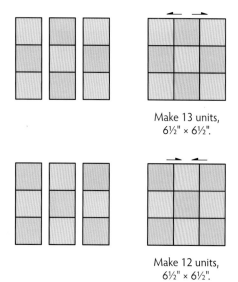

Make 13 units,
6½" × 6½".

Make 12 units,
6½" × 6½".

5. Sew two print 2½" × 5½" rectangles together end to end to make a pieced strip. Press. Repeat to make a total of 50 pieced strips.

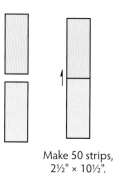

Make 50 strips,
2½" × 10½".

6. Sew two pieced strips to the sides of a nine-patch unit to make a block. Press. The block should measure 10½" square, including seam allowances. Repeat to make a total of 25 blocks.

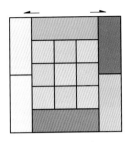

Make 13 blocks, 10½" × 10½".

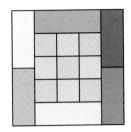

Make 12 blocks, 10½" × 10½".

Assembling the Quilt Top

1. Lay out the blocks in five rows of five, rotating the blocks in each row as shown in the quilt assembly diagram below.

2. Sew the blocks into rows. Press.

3. Sew the rows together. Press.

Finishing the Quilt

If you need more instructions for any of the following steps, download free information at ShopMartingale.com/HowtoQuilt.

1. Cut the backing fabric into two 1⅝-yard lengths. Remove the selvages and sew the pieces together side by side, referring to "How to Piece a Quilt Backing" on page 10. Press the seam allowances to one side.

2. Layer and baste the backing, batting, and quilt top. Quilt as desired. The quilt shown was machine quilted across its width with wavy lines, providing a counterpoint to the straight lines of the piecing.

3. Trim the batting and backing even with the edges of the quilt top.

4. Using the red 2½"-wide strips, make double-fold binding and attach it to the quilt.

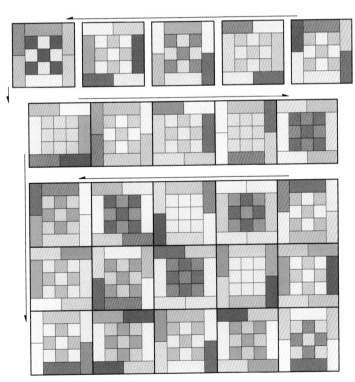

Quilt assembly

FINISHED QUILT: 41" × 41"   •   FINISHED BLOCK: 9½" × 9½"

Cross My Heart

BY AMY HAMBERLIN; QUILTED BY JENNIFER MCCLANAHAN ● ● ● ● ● ● ● ● ●

Snowball blocks are easy to make with the sew-and-flip corner technique. And if the Plus Sign blocks look tricky to insert, don't worry—they're really just squares and rectangles in the sashing. So pick a collection of favorite fat quarters and get ready to have some fun with this sweet quilt.

Materials

Yardage is based on 42"-wide fabric. Fat quarters measure 18" × 21". Fat eighths measure 9" × 21".

1¼ yards of cream print for block backgrounds and sashing

9 fat eighths of assorted check for Snowball blocks

6 fat quarters of assorted prints for Plus Sign blocks

½ yard of aqua print for binding

3 yards of fabric for backing

49" × 49" piece of batting

Cutting

All measurements include ¼" seam allowances.

From the cream print, cut:

10 strips, 2½" × 42"; crosscut into:

    12 strips, 2½" × 10"

    24 strips, 2½" × 6"

    40 squares, 2½" × 2½"

8 strips, 1½" × 42"; crosscut into:

    18 strips, 1½" × 10"

    18 strips, 1½" × 8"

From *each* checked fat quarter, cut:

1 square, 8" × 8"

From *each* print fat quarter, cut:

3 strips, 2½" × 6½" (18 total)

6 squares, 2½" × 2½" (36 total)

From the aqua print, cut:

5 strips, 2½" × 42"

Making the Blocks

Press all seam allowances as indicated by the arrows in the illustrations.

1. Draw a diagonal line on the wrong side of 36 cream 2½" squares.

2. Place a marked cream square on each corner of a checked 8" square, right sides together as shown. Sew on the drawn lines. Trim away the excess fabric, leaving a ¼" seam allowance. Press. The unit should measure 8" square, including seam allowances. Repeat to make a total of nine units.

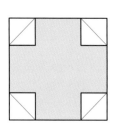 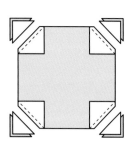

Make 9 units,
8" × 8".

3. Sew cream 1½" × 8" strips to the top and bottom of a step 2 unit. Press. Sew a cream 1½" × 10" strip to each side to make a Snowball block. Press. The block should measure 10" square, including seam allowances. Repeat to make a total of nine blocks.

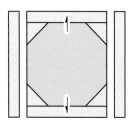 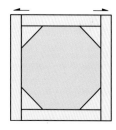

Make 9 blocks,
10" × 10".

Assembling the Quilt Top

1. Referring to the assembly diagram on page 63, lay out the Snowball blocks, cream 2½" × 6" and 2½" × 10" strips, cream 2½" squares, and print 2½" × 6½" strips and 2½" squares, matching the print rectangles and squares to form plus signs as shown.

QUICK DESIGN WALL

Laying out the pieces for your quilt is easy when you have a design wall. All you need is a length of flannel or batting—or you can use the flannel backing of a vinyl tablecloth. Pin your flannel or batting to a wall or lay it on the floor, then arrange your blocks and other fabric pieces on the surface. The fabrics will stick, but they're also easy to rearrange as you experiment with placement options.

2. Before you can sew the pieces together into rows, you'll need to make the sashing units. To do this, remove two print 2½" squares and one cream 2½" × 6" strip from the layout and sew them together to make one vertical sashing unit as shown. Press. The unit should measure 2½" × 10", including seam allowances. Place the unit back into the layout. Make a total of 12 vertical sashing units.

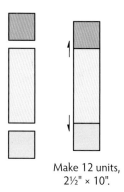

Make 12 units,
2½" × 10".

3. Sew the pieces into horizontal rows. Press the seam allowances toward the print squares and rectangles in rows 1, 2, 4, 6, 8, and 9 as indicated by the arrows. Press the seam allowances toward the blocks and cream strips in rows 3, 5, and 7.

4. Sew the rows together. Press the seam allowances toward rows 2, 4, 6, and 8 to complete the quilt top.

Finishing the Quilt

If you need more instructions for any of the following steps, download free information at ShopMartingale.com/HowtoQuilt.

1. Cut the backing fabric into two 1½-yard lengths. Remove the selvages and sew the pieces together side by side, referring to "How to Piece a Quilt Backing" on page 10. Press the seam allowances to one side.

2. Layer and baste the backing, batting, and quilt top. Quilt as desired. The quilt shown is machine quilted with an allover pattern of swirls and leaves.

3. Trim the batting and backing even with the edges of the quilt top.

4. Using the aqua 2½"-wide strips, make double-fold binding and attach it to the quilt.

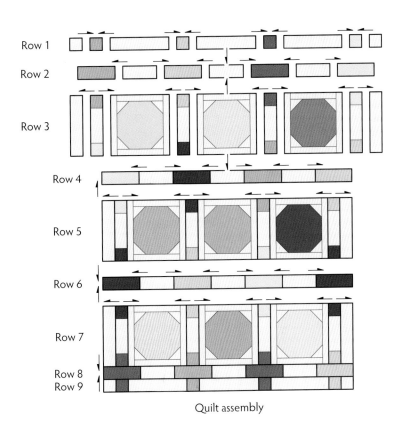

Quilt assembly

About the Contributors

Melissa Corry

Melissa began quilting as a hobby in 2002 and started a blog in 2010. Her hobby has become a passion that she shares through tutorials, patterns, and her book, *Irish Chain Quilts* (Martingale, 2015). You can visit Melissa at HappyQuiltingMelissa.com.

Kim Diehl

With just the third quilt she'd ever made, self-taught quiltmaker Kim Diehl became the winner of *American Patchwork & Quilting* magazine's "Pieces of the Past" quilt challenge in 1998, turning her life onto a new and unexpected path. Her work has been featured in numerous national and international quilting magazines. In addition to her best-selling "Simple" series of quilting books published with Martingale, Kim has designed several fabric collections for Henry Glass & Co., enabling her to be involved in the full circle of quiltmaking from start to finish.

Amy Ellis

Amy was amazed to discover the great source of inspiration and abundance of knowledge that makes up the blogging world, and decided to become part of it via Amy's Creative Side, where she shares current projects (including quilts, bags, and the occasional garment), product reviews, and little bits of her family life as a wife and mother. She hosts a biannual Bloggers' Quilt Festival, where there's no judging or required skill set for entry, so it's more like a big party online! Amy is the author of five books and contributor to many more. Visit her at AmysCreativeSide.com.

Amy Hamberlin

Amy made her first quilt when she was pregnant with her daughter. She was looking for the perfect crib set and couldn't find it, so decided to make her own. While making that first quilt, she fell in love with quilting. Years later, she opened her own quilt shop. Currently Amy designs quilts and bags. Visit her at KatiCupcake.bigcartel.com.

Kimberly Jolly

Kimberly is the owner of Fat Quarter Shop, an online fabric store, and It's Sew Emma, a pattern company. Her designs are often inspired by vintage quilts and blocks, but she occasionally ventures out to try something new. Kimberly loves to create quilts for friends and family, especially her children, who are a constant source of inspiration.

Sue Pfau

Sue first started quilting as a flight attendant, bringing hand appliqué on flights. In 2006 she began making and selling quilts but had a hard time finding patterns that were quick and easy yet also beautiful and interesting. So she began designing her own. This led to her design company, called Sweet Jane's Quilting and Design after her daughter, Jane, who was adopted from China. (Her son, Jack, was adopted from Taiwan.) Visit Sue at SweetJanesQuilting.blogspot.com.

Piper's Girls

Piper's Girls is a quilting, sewing, and knitting design team that runs an online shop and hosts pop-up classes and shopping events in and around Salt Lake City, Utah. Erin Hamilton and Jeanette White are the Piper's Girls. The two specialize in children's and baby items but also dabble in a bit of everything. They hope their designs make you smile. Visit Piper's Girls at PipersGirls.com.

Vicki Ruebel

Vicki specializes in custom freehand quilting and computerized edge-to-edge quilting. Her award-winning quilts lean toward a contemporary aesthetic. She has contributed many original designs to *Make Modern* magazine and *Modern Quilts Unlimited*. She enjoys teaching and encouraging others to find their quilting voice. Visit Vicki at OrchidOwlQuilts.com.

Krystal Stahl

Krystal is part of the It's Sew Emma team and has dived into the quilting world with both feet. Combining her graphic design background with an eye for aesthetics, she enjoys designing quilts with a modern slant.